ALL ORGANIZING IS DIS-ORGANIZING AND RE-ORGANIZING

FREEDOM FROM
and
FREEDOM FOR

Michael Gecan

acta
PUBLICATIONS

FREEDOM FROM AND FREEDOM FOR
by Michael Gecan

Edited by Gregory F. Augustine Pierce
Cover and text design and typesetting by Patricia A. Lynch

Copyright © 2011 by Michael Gecan

Published by ACTA Publications, 4848 N. Clark St., Chicago, IL 60640, (800) 397-2282, www.actapublications.com

All rights reserved. No part of this publication may be reproduced or transmitted in any form or by any means, electronic or mechanical, including photocopying and recording, or by any information storage and retrieval system, including the Internet, without permission from the publisher. Permission is hereby given to use short excerpts or pieces of art with proper citation in reviews and marketing copy, church bulletins and handouts, and scholarly papers.

ISBN: 978-0-87946-465-3
Printed in the United States of America by Total Printing Systems
Year 20 19 18 17 16 15 14 13 12 11
Printing 15 14 13 12 11 10 9 8 7 6 5 4 3 2 First

✪ Text printed on 30% post-consumer recycled paper

A NOTE FROM THE PUBLISHER

★★★★

No one in public life in America is more thoughtful than Mike Gecan. He has earned the right to his political opinions through a lifetime of organizing people to take control of their own lives and communities. It was Gecan who went into East Brooklyn in the early 1980s and instead of accepting the hopelessness and devastation he found there he envisioned a rebuilt community controlled by its residents. He organized the East Brooklyn Churches to make that vision a reality through the Nehemiah Project, which built 5,000 single-family, owner occupied townhomes that transformed not only that community but also how community organizing is done in the United States.

Now as the co-executive director of the Industrial Areas Foundation and Metro IAF, Gecan oversees many of the top community organizations in the country. He has also become a well-respected spokesperson and author about democracy with his books *Going Public*, *After America's Midlife Crisis*, and *Effective Organizing for Congregational Renewal*.

With this essay, Gecan looks at the question of freedom in America society, differentiating between *freedom from* and *freedom for*. Refusing to buy into the current liberal-conservative stereotypes, he argues that both freedoms are vital to the functioning of democracy and predicts that unless the moderate ideological middle of American society—including its religious institutions—recognizes the value and fights for both freedoms, our future as a civil society might be lost.

Of special interest is Gecan's analysis of the political instincts of the Tea Party and other groups who are considered by many progressives to be mean-spirited and anti-democratic. Gecan claims, instead, that many in conservative movements are motivated by a genuine desire to be left alone by the government whenever possible and to take responsibility for their own lives and communities.

So while *Freedom From and Freedom For* is not a prescription for where we need to go as a country, it does raise the right issues and invite serious dialogue. I urge you to read it in that spirit.

> Gregory F. Augustine Pierce
> President and Co-Publisher
> ACTA Publications

INTRODUCTION

★★★★

ALL ORGANIZING IS DIS-ORGANIZING AND RE-ORGANIZING

*One belief,
more than any other,
is responsible for the slaughter of individuals
on the altars of the great historical ideals.*

Isaiah Berlin

One bitter January morning my wife, Sheila, and I were walking through the main quad of the University of Georgia. We were in Athens for a family celebration and wanted to get a feel for the campus and the town. It was early, and the quad was empty and still, except for a party of intrepid Chinese parents and a small but energetic group of students taking photos at the famous Arch.

To our left, near the Arch, we found ourselves in front of the Holmes-Hunter Building, renamed in the year 2000 to honor Charlayne Hunter-Gault and the late Dr. Hamilton Holmes, the first two African American students to enroll in the school in 1961. The university president, Michael Adams, said at the time: "Their courageous act paved the way for the University of Georgia to be an educational institution that serves all citizens. Naming this building for them ensures that their personal contributions will never be forgotten."

Right across the walk from the building was a plaque that briefly described the history of the university – founded in 1785, closed in 1864 and 1865 because most students and staff were away, fighting in what the plaque's creator called "The War for Southern Independence."

In that compact space, in the names on the building and the words on the plaque, in the capacity of that campus to present two very different faces to the world, we felt that we had wandered into some special place.

A few months after our University of Georgia experience, Nicholas Kristof put that feeling into words in a piece he wrote praising the late Isaiah Berlin on the anniversary of Berlin's one hundredth birthday. He admired Berlin's ability to find and explore "the boundary between what can be tolerated with gritted teeth and what is morally intolerable." When I read that phrase – "what can be tolerated with gritted teeth" – I imagined how some would walk by the Hunter-Holmes building with gritted teeth, while others would have the same reaction to the sign that described the Civil War as "the War for Southern Independence."

Berlin wrote wonderfully on many topics, but one of his greatest essays, "Two Concepts of Liberty," includes this insight: "One belief, more than any other, is responsible for the slaughter of individuals on the altars of the great historical ideals.... This is the belief that somewhere, in the past or in the future, in the divine revelation or in the mind of an individual thinker, in the pronouncements of history or science, or in the simple heart of an uncorrupted good man, there is a final solution. This ancient faith rests on the conviction that all the positive values in which men have believed must, in the end, be compatible, and perhaps even entail one another."

Berlin argued instead for the notion of "negative freedom" or "negative liberty." It is *freedom from*. "The desire to be governed by myself, or at any rate to participate in the process by which my life is to be controlled, may be as deep a wish as that for a free area for action, and perhaps historically older," he wrote. The desire for *freedom from* is as deep, as recurring, as persistent, as the power of what poet Wallace Stevens called "April's green." And it is older than the founding of our nation.

The first European in America to organize to be *free from* the control of someone else was Adrian von der Donck. Writer Russell Shorto, in his book *The Island at the Center of the World*, described how von der Donck persuaded his neighbors in New Amsterdam to go door to door and resist what he considered the abuses of the heavy-handed Peter Stuyvesant. Von der Donck was no peacenik. He had already served as the sheriff of the wilderness settlement that later became the city of Albany. He had sailed up the Hudson just twenty years after the great captain first explored it. I rode up that same wide river one August recently, in an Amtrak club car on my way to Montreal. It was a warm, overcast summer morning. Low wooded hills still border the river, just as they did when von der Donck sailed north. The contrast between this vast unrolling expanse of river and forest and the compact and cultivated fields and canals of his native country must have been even more stunning to him than it is to us today. Von der Donck came from a place of fixed physical limits, where every square foot of arable land had to be forcefully and artfully reclaimed from the sea, where water was the primary reality, where getting along with others was as critical to a Dutch burgher in the seventeenth century as it is to a New York subway rider in the twenty-first. Then he found himself in a place where fields and forests, space seemingly beyond measure, room to roam, replaced water as the primary reality. He wrote about it all with great feeling and craft.

In the 1640s, von der Donck had moved back downriver to New Amsterdam, and he and his fellow New Amsterdamers met one to one with their neighbors. They prepared a portfolio of issues and concerns. And they took their grievances to the ultimate authority at the time – which happened to be an ocean and a season away, in The Netherlands. Von der Donck had limited goals – some form of participation in public life, restraint of Stuyvesant's abuse of power, grudging acceptance of certain minimal rights. Russell Shorto defines it as simply being "put up with." Centuries of struggle with the power and pressure of the sea had conditioned him. Along with so many wonderful names – Brooklyn,

Yonkers, the Bronx, the Tappan Zee – von der Donck and his fellow citizens transported to us this appreciation of perpetual interaction and incremental adjustments, of limitation and modesty in the public sphere, of extended time frames and long horizons.

Freedom from is the older and less charismatic sibling in the family of freedoms. *Freedom for* – positive liberty – arrived later, but has attracted more attention and perhaps more affection than the first-born form. That's why, in this essay, I will give *freedom from* its due, before trying to describe how this family of freedoms functions well together.

Michael Gecan
Princeton, New Jersey
May 1, 2011

FREEDOM FROM AND FREEDOM FOR

★★★★

*The fundamental sense of freedom
is freedom from chains,
from imprisonment,
from enslavement by others.*

Isaiah Berlin

Not long ago, I was in Rock Falls, Illinois, in the far western part of the state, getting ready to conduct a training session for organizers and staff affiliated with the teachers' association there. It was a blisteringly hot stretch, at least eighty degrees by dawn. I woke early and realized that I had time to take a drive to a nearby town, Tampico, where Ronald Reagan was born. The fields were already alive with farm workers, dressed heavily to ward off the damp, their yellow transport bus parked along the road. A church spire and water tower rose above the trees ahead. A sign – "The Churches of Tampico welcome you…pop: 800" – announced the way to town, which was one street, crossed diagonally by a train track.

On one side of the street were the Tampico Farmers Elevator, Inc; a medical office (Hasmukh Shah, MD); a faded wooden feed house; an historical museum; the

Garlan Funeral Home; the First National Bank building, on the second floor of which is the apartment where Ronald Reagan lived with his family until the age of nine or so; Poston's Market; and the Dutch Diner. Across the street, in front of the Tampico Bank Center, was a boulder sporting a plaque. The plaque instructed that Ronald Reagan was born in Tampico on February 6, 1911. Nearby Dixon, Illinois, where the Reagans stayed longer, captures most of the tourist traffic. But it was right here, in unlikely Tampico, across the street from the deserted and deteriorating Pitney Store, that young Ronald Reagan got his start. Across the rail line, in Ronald Reagan Park, an artillery piece aims skyward.

I hadn't had coffee, so asked the two men sitting on a bench at 6:30 AM in front of Poston's Market if I could get a cup there. One of the gents, in his fifties, the owner, ushered me inside and asked me to help myself. He was a devoted Chicago Bears fan, so we talked football for a while. I mentioned that I now lived in New Jersey, and he described that two sisters from New Jersey had moved into town a few years ago "and stayed." It seemed to surprise him a bit. The other fellow, called Sarge, a World War II vet, stayed outside and watched the street.

The *modesty* of the place – small, rural, declining now – struck me. In a sea of farmland, that began about 400 miles east in Ohio and ended perhaps 800 miles west in Colorado, sat Tampico, its few families in homes built on a human scale on streets that ran a few blocks and then ended abruptly at the edge of acres of soybeans and corn. They looked out and saw the vastness and richness of the surrounding land. They looked up and watched clouds fill a sprawling sky. Later that afternoon, a violent thunderstorm rolled in, darkened the lights in the Falls River hotel and left splintered trees and flooded fields all across the region.

Lincoln's homestead in Springfield, which I also visited a few months earlier, also had the same affect on me as Tampico. Not only is his home preserved, but so are the homes around it. You have a sense of what the neighborhood looked and felt like when Lincoln and his family lived there in the years before he became our nation's greatest president. I didn't get to his home until after closing time. I stood outside, with a family of four, also late. As we began to drift away, a park ranger emerged from the home and spotted us. She asked us if we wanted to take a quick tour and then led us on an informative thirty-minute walk-through.

The relatively young political figure who once lived there had spent his youth moving from Kentucky to Indiana to Illinois, earning his living by the sweat of his brow, quite literally, and having his earnings appropriated by his father. His sensitivity to all attacks on the value of labor and the patient building of equity – his deeply ingrained sense of fairness – developed during those early years. But they were reflected on and refined, in letters and speeches, as he sat at this desk, in this chair, in these rooms, in this normal, mixed, troubled, full, complex family setting. Just months after he packed up his goods and moved to Washington, after a farewell speech to his Springfield neighbors, he would say, in his July 4, 1861, message to Congress: "This is essentially a People's contest. On the one side of the Union, it is a struggle for maintaining in the world that form and substance of government whose leading object is to elevate the condition of man; to lift artificial weights from all shoulders; to clear the paths of laudable pursuit for all; to afford all an unfettered start and a fair chance in the race of life."

This is such a fine and mature and subtle expression of a political vision. It is, like the Midwest itself, both grand and limited. The words *elevate*, *lift*, and *all* (repeated three times), convey how grand Lincoln's political vision was. But his word *laudable* conveys that not all pursuits are equal. Instead of expanding that form and substance of government, his goal is *maintaining* it. Rather than guaranteeing victory or even equality of outcome, he believes that the role of government is to afford *unfettered start, and a fair chance* in the race of life. And life remains, for Lincoln, a competition, an exertion, a struggle, a *race*. You must be free to run, but run you must, with no guarantee of where you will eventually place, because others are running and running hard.

A century later, Isaiah Berlin would write: "The fundamental sense of freedom is freedom from chains, from imprisonment, from enslavement by others. The rest is extension of this sense, or else metaphor. To strive to be free is to seek to remove obstacles; to struggle for personal freedom is to seek to curb interference, exploitation, enslavement by men whose ends are theirs, not one's own. Freedom, at least in its political sense, is coterminous with the absence of bullying or domination.... Emphasis on negative liberty, as a rule, leaves more paths for individuals or groups to pursue; positive liberty, as a rule, opens fewer paths, but with better reasons or greater resources for moving them along; the two may or may not clash."

As the Civil War progressed, as the casualties mounted, as the resources of the nation were consumed, as the cost of removing obstacles rose, Lincoln needed to use more and more governmental power to achieve his limited ends. To guarantee negative liberty (*freedom from*) to all, he had to move deeper into the field of positive liberty (*freedom for*). Historian James McPherson described this shift: "But beginning with the Thirteenth Amendment in 1865 – the amendment that abolished slavery – six of the next seven amendments radically expanded the power of the federal government at the expense of the states.... Power in these cases expanded liberty instead of repressing it; power and liberty were allies, not enemies. The emphasis was not on freedom from, but freedom to. These amendments...define *into* the population enjoying certain rights and liberties large groups that had been previously defined *out*: black people and women.... Abraham Lincoln played a crucial role in this historic shift of emphasis from negative liberty to positive liberty." That's why McPherson aptly titled his book, *Abraham Lincoln and the Second American Revolution*.

This was a risky and revolutionary shift. Negative liberty (*freedom from*) was hard-wired into the political program of our republic. "The Bill of Rights," as McPherson has pointed out, "is an excellent example of negative liberty. Nearly all of the first ten amendments to the Constitution apply the phrase 'shall not' to the federal government. In fact, eleven of the first twelve amendments placed limitations on the power of the national government." The basic posture of the citizens of this new republic was *defensive*. At times, they needed to rally, grudgingly, after other options had been tried, to defend that limited government against other, worse forms of government. But, once free of the crown or clerics or other forms of tyranny, they had to be just as wary of their own government.

"The doctrine that accumulations of power can never be too great, provided that they are rationally controlled and used, ignores the central reason for pursuing liberty in the first place – *that all paternalistic governments, however benevolent, cautious, disinterested, and rational, have tended, in the end, to treat the majority of men as minors, or as being too often incurably foolish or irresponsible; or else as maturing so slowly as not to justify their liberation at any clearly foreseeable date (which, in practice, means at no definite time at all). This is a policy which degrades men, and seems to me to rest on no rational or scientific foundation, but, on the contrary, on a profoundly mistaken view of the deepest human needs.*" (Isaiah Berlin, italics mine)

The founders of the American experiment were

emerging out of several hundred years of catastrophic war, colonization, and repression. Final solutions proposed and enforced by monarchs and clerics had decimated both the old and new worlds. The general populace knew little else than subjugation and control. *Freedom from* might not seem like such a lofty goal to many citizens of the twenty-first century. But just being left alone, being free to buy and sell goods in a more open market, being free to come to conclusions about the nature of the universe without imprisonment or banishment or worse, were, as Leszek Kolakowski wrote in *The Idolatry of Politics*, "…a side of the same centuries-long process whereby the modern idea of negative freedom and the principles of freedom of economic activity and of legal equality were established. Market economics, rationalist philosophy, liberal political doctrines and institutions, and modern science emerged as interconnected aspects of the same evolution, *and none of them could have asserted itself separately* (italics mine)." The American Revolution was a *freedom from* moment. Abraham Lincoln, the unlikely leader of *freedom for*, the second American revolution, came of age when veterans of the first still lived, when the stories and memories of the overthrow of British rule were both fresh and raw.

The desire to be *free from* is not a mere *interest*; it is deeper than that – perhaps the core of our national character and an ingrained cultural reflex. It may be quintessentially, fundamentally, what it means to be an American. Modern progressives tut-tut when moderates and conservatives seem to "vote against their own interests." But this should come as no surprise. People are voting for, or responding to, this instinct, or a set of instincts. They are saying "shall not" in their own way and in their own time. They are defending themselves from the smugness and superiority of the high priests of academia and the royalist tendencies of the political and media elites. They may even be asserting that they will accept the damage done when *freedom from* allows market forces to sap equity, destroy credit ratings, close offices and plants, profit from widespread foreclosures, and bankrupt scores of millions because they believe that the harm implicit in the *freedom for* path could well be greater. The *freedom from* instinct may not be uninformed or misinformed, as progressives like to claim. History has shown that we all have a right to remain wary.

So "local control" is *freedom from*. "No new taxes" is *freedom from*. Resisting "big government" and expansive federal programs is *freedom from*. Restraining regulation of the market is *freedom from*. These themes literally strike chords in many Americans – including the majority of Americans, who are moderate – not just those on the right. (Strangely, the emphasis on a free and highly subsidized press in the first seventy-five years of the nation's history was another product of the powerful drive to be free from domination by centralized interests. The Founding Fathers almost unanimously agreed on the need for federal support, through the postal service, of the distribution and delivery of papers and periodicals. Communication and information needed to be available and affordable to all, including those in the most remote locations, so that citizens had the information that could equip them to resist those who used slanted or withheld information as an instrument of control. In other words, the Founders made a judgment that significant government intervention and long-term funding, in the name of *freedom from*, was appropriate and justified.)

Conservatives seem to have a better ear for this. And "ear" might be the right way to describe this. This instinct or reflex is as much music as text, as much rhythm as narrative. It is not less serious or real than a position that can be written or verbalized. It just means that it exists, quite literally, on a different wavelength.

Political leaders and opinion drivers on the right hear these echoes more clearly and both chant and respond to them more creatively. But just because the conservatives exploit this cultural tendency doesn't make the reflex wrong, or, at the very least, not worthy of understanding and respect. In fact, every time progressives decry the drive to be *free from*, they try to drown out a theme that many Americans resonate with. When conservative pundits call progressives "un-American," they are onto something. And progressives who insist on dismissing the theme of free men and free markets just demonstrate again that they are tone deaf.

Many people have commented on how rapidly Lincoln aged during this presidency. The usual explanation is the human toll of the Civil War, the butcher's bill that grew and grew until it totaled 623,000 casualties. Of course the cost in lives lost wore Lincoln down. But the energy expended by the president in this extraordinary pivot – from a tradition of *freedom from* that he both understood and revered to a commitment to *freedom for* – must have been an excruciating intellectual exercise. He knew what he was up against, not just on the battlefield, or in the Congress, or with the international community. He knew that the moment had come where *freedom from*, negative liberty for some, had evolved into another kind of despotism. "Southern slaveholders," wrote McPherson, "had exercised their asserted liberty of self-government to protect their 'liberty of making slaves of other people,' as Lincoln had once put it sarcastically." Overcoming that despotism required overwhelming government intervention and a series of forceful actions that expanded the body politic and the tendency toward positive liberty or *freedom for*. And there, he may have known and felt, lay a whole new set of other dangers for our republic.

Every revolution generates forms of resistance, even counter-revolutions. After the Civil War and Reconstruction, southern states reasserted their "liberty of self-government" to deny blacks the right to vote, the right to an equal education, the right to life itself in some cases. A white acquaintance of mine who was a young girl on the day in 1954 that the Supreme Court ruled on *Brown vs. Board of Education* recalls a gathering of people in her small Georgia town. She was too young to understand the issues at stake. But she could feel the deep fear and anxiety in her parents and their white neighbors that evening in the square. Seven years later, the University of Georgia admitted its first two African American students. Fifty-four years later, the nation elected its first African American president. And while hundreds of thousands of Americans packed Grant Park on election night and the nation's Capitol on inauguration day, and many millions more laughed and sang and cried with joy and astonishment all across the country, there were also towns and neighborhoods and communities where other Americans, also in the millions, greeted this seismic political and social shift with gritted teeth.

A new kind of political geography would produce maps that traced all the fault lines where negative (*freedom from*) and positive (*freedom for*) liberty scrape against one another, collide, and cause eruptions. I didn't know it at the time, but I grew up on one such fault line in the west side of my Chicago hometown and felt the impact. Most attention gets focused on the summers of outbreaks on the west and south sides of the city in the later 1960s. And those days and nights were certainly dramatic and memorable. One evening, coming home on the Lake Street el, with fellow Chicagoans who were black and white, bullets hit our train as we passed by the Henry Horner Homes during an outbreak. All of us hit the floor, black and white together, in an intense and instant moment of survivor solidarity. At the next station, cops and national guard troops were out in force, firing back at the darkened public housing projects in the distance, ushering us down to buses waiting below. We were driven through the streets, with fires and firing outside. The blacks got off at "their" stops. We whites got off, several blocks beyond, at "ours."

These explosions of violence followed decades of smaller rumbles. In my neighborhood, West Garfield Park, no young black person could walk through without being harassed, chased, and, if caught, beaten badly. If we heard that a black gang planned to make an incursion, we would gather in our basements and make homemade bombs, collect bats and bricks, and deploy ourselves at the points near the Chicago and Northwestern tracks and viaducts where we expected our foes to cross. Of course, the reverse was also true. If we wandered south of Madison in the 1950s and then Lake Street in the 1960s and then the railroad tracks even later, we could expect the same response. The difference was we didn't want "their" homes or parks or schools. But they, we believed, very much wanted "ours." Our desire to be "free" meant freedom from black home buyers, black neighbors, black school children in our schools and parishes and playgrounds.

★★★★

In Milwaukee, ninety miles north, considered even more segregated and racially troubled than Chicago, similar scenes occurred in the 1960s. As I rode through the streets one sunny Sunday recently, looking at areas ravaged by the recent wave of foreclosures, I saw large frame homes that often looked half-empty, structures in need of roofing, carpentry work, new stairs, modern windows. This wasn't the dramatic decline that once scarred the South Bronx or East Brooklyn and still makes swaths of Chicago south and west sides look so grim. Milwaukee's homes are bigger, less dense, detached, with yards in front and back. This wasn't the sound and smell of the nightly fires that burned cities in the 1960s. Here was the steady smoldering of the 2000s – consuming communities slowly and relentlessly. The commercial streets looked listless, or empty. The former manufacturing plants and warehouses were bricked up. In this already weakened city, the foreclosure map on the seat of my car showed which blocks were about to endure even more distress.

The whites who had once occupied these homes – Italians, Irish, German, Slovak, Czech, Croatian, and others – had defeated the Axis powers in World War II. They had fought against the most grotesque extension of the concept of positive liberty (*freedom for*) that the world had yet seen. They had fought for *freedom from* – freedom to be left alone by the totalitarians on the left and right who had sought to eradicate the human person and all mediating institutions in the name of the party or the state or the Führer or the race. They had liberated oppressed and enslaved people by the millions. They had killed their own countryman in the process

– Milwaukee and Chicago Germans fighting their own kinsmen on the other side of the line, immigrant Croatians like my father fighting Croatians who were often willing parts of the Nazi machine.

Then they had come home to their wives and children, their bungalows and two-flats, their factory jobs and corner bars, their parishes and schools, and just wanted to be left alone. They wanted to be free from the blacks across the tracks, from the liberal lawyers and professors pushing integration, from the federal agencies looking for sites for public housing for the poor, from the do-gooders and social workers. It felt to them as if a larger and more powerful set of forces was trying to dictate to them the terms of the very public life that they had just fought to preserve. And they – and I would have to say "we," because I was part of this world as a young person – reacted.

Of course, the blacks across the tracks had fought or served in World War II as well, or worked in the plants while others were overseas. Many of them had also bled to free others. And now they wanted to be free as well – from the tenements and loan sharks, ghetto rats and inflated rents, the lousy schools and third-rate services that they were accustomed to. They wanted what we whites wanted – a decent home, a job, a good school for the kids, a yard, a car, and mostly to be left alone.

The cost of this nationally – millions of families multiply relocating, trillions of dollars lost as whites sold low and bought higher and blacks bought high and sold lower, thousands of neighborhoods gutted, entire denominations left with empty buildings and shuttered schools, a generation of infrastructure built for living communities now rusting liabilities for struggling ones, hundreds of cities weakened and then shattered – is beyond calculation and still mounting today.

I've seen no signs similar to the plaques in Athens, Georgia, on the deserted and dying streets of Chicago and Milwaukee. There was no plaque celebrating the day the first black family moved into Sherman Park in Milwaukee or West Garfield Park in Chicago. There was no marker commemorating the white families who stayed and related and created working class communities that included both whites and blacks.

At a training session for public sector union leaders, one of the participants asked me what I thought of the rise of the Tea Party. The questioner assumed that I would be as disturbed as he was.

I told the group that I thought that this was a healthy development. I felt that it was far better for people to step onto the public stage and try to explain and promote and defend their views. In the process, other people get a chance to engage them, relate to them, challenge them, *and be challenged by them.*

There was an uneasy silence for a while. Then, in the back, I noticed a woman, about 45 and a long-time member of the union and its staff, who had half-raised her hand. I asked her if she wanted to make a comment. She hesitated, said she wasn't quite sure. After a little encouragement, she confessed, "Well, I'm not sure that I should admit this here, but I recently attended a Tea Party meeting." More uneasy silence. I asked why she decided to go. "Well, I saw that all my neighbors were going. And they aren't crazy. So I got curious and decided I should too." She described it as nothing out of the ordinary – what any union or citizens organization would call a typical house meeting.

I asked the group if anyone else had attended a Tea Party event. Not a hand or a nod. Then I went after them a bit by suggesting that this is a major problem. Most people attracted to the Tea Party movements are not ideologues or extremists. They are neighbors and co-workers. They are the parents who send their kids to local schools and the families filling church pews. They are the people in the middle, some more right, some more left, who are feeling profound anxiety about their jobs and their communities, about their ability to pay their mortgages or credit cards, about how to cover tuition costs for their children or find affordable care for their elderly parents. And those generating the Tea Party momentum are doing what those on the left have long thought was their sole possession: old-fashioned, grassroots, local organizing. (When a reporter once called and asked what Saul Alinsky, the founder of citizens organizing in the United States, would have said about the Tea Party people using his name and studying his approach, I responded, "Oh, Saul would have been appalled. Everyone knows that democracy is only for the left." The reporter chose not to quote me.)

It would be just as wrong to assume that those in the middle have been captured by the right as it would be to assume that they have been captured by the left. Being in the middle doesn't mean that people are moderate. It means that they have a mix of views and perspectives based on a rich range of experiences and instincts, not an internally consistent set of predictable positions.

Almost every other time I've tried to make this point, the immediate reaction is for someone who is progressive to say: "But they are all racists." I always ask the person how many Tea Party people they know, how many meetings or events they've attended, how many hours have they spent listening to the fears and anxieties of these men and women. The answer is almost always none. They know no one in this group. They've been to nothing. They've not listened to anyone. They take their cues from liberal pundits and from surfing the Internet. Of course, those on the right often do the same thing – using conservative pundits and websites as their prophets and texts. Are some on the right racists? Sure. Is everyone? Of course not. Are some on the left elitists? You bet. Is everyone? Let's hope not.

We are a long way from what Nicholas Kristol called "the boundary between what can be tolerated with gritted teeth and what is morally intolerable." In fact, we are back to the kind of pitched, bitter, polarized battles that took place all along the racial fault-lines in hundreds of American cities from the 1960s through the 1980s. The modern Tea Party is the suburban and western descendant of that movement of mostly white working class residents that sought, in their minds, to preserve neighborhood stability and to protect their hard-earned equity and security from sinking property values and rising crime. The battle isn't in physical space these days — not street by street and block by block. It's in political space, and it is fought over more abstract issues of taxation and regulation and heritage. The intact and stable and exclusive nation has replaced the intact and stable and exclusive neighborhood as the wall to be defended to the death.

In both cases, there has been little or no exploration of the boundary area, of the space between the two extremes, where most Americans still live and operate. Until there is, there is no way that public relationships can be built or deepened — relationships that don't depend upon ideological uniformity and complete agreement but upon a full and respectful understanding of *who* people are, of *why* they think in different ways, of *how* their different experiences and struggles have led them in different conclusions. Without that foundation of public relationships, it's impossible to step out and test what can be tolerated with gritted teeth and what is morally unacceptable. The America that de Tocqueville found when he traveled, a young man in a young nation in the 1831 and 1832, a world of seemingly spontaneous and endless associations, is in danger of disappearing. What that union member from central Illinois did in attending a Tea Party meeting to learn what it is all about is now a very rare exception, not the norm of our public life.

The new norm is not to engage, not to venture out into the no-man's-land between the two main camps. This is not just a natural evolution in our country. Nor, in my mind, is it a conspiracy. It's worse than that. It's becoming *the dominant culture* in the U.S. public arena. And it's a culture of ideological division that has traction because it happens to serve – and be served by – a wide range of powerful institutional interests.

★★★★

The same was true in the days of "changing neighborhoods" in Chicago. There could have been many more instances of neighborhoods and communities that integrated successfully over time, like suburban Oak Park and Evanston on the borders of Chicago, or Hyde Park on the south side. But it was very much in the interest of the real estate and financial establishments – brokers, title companies, mortgage companies, banks, assessors, lawyers, and others – for neighborhood after neighborhood to re-segregate from white to black or white to Hispanic. The volume and pace of neighborhood change translated into profits for the city's insiders. The real estate-related professions used a percentage of those profits to underwrite the Cook County Democratic Party. A percentage of every transaction, mortgage, title fee, legal charge made its way into the coffers of the Machine. When the racial make-up of an area changed, the Machine supported white lackeys for as long as possible and then selected minority lackeys to replace them.

These institutions thrived while small civic groups fought pitched and losing battles to keep new minority residents out. The new residents lost too, inheriting communities with reduced services, struggling schools, and emptying commercial strips. Small businesses often followed their ethnic customers out to the first ring of suburbs and newer suburban tracts. More than 800,000 people fled, leaving a city of 3.6 million with just 2.8 million residents today – 75% of the former population of Chicago supporting 100% of the streets, sewers, water and school systems, and police and fire departments. (The finest account of this process has been written by Beryl Satter, in her book *Family Properties*.)

Nationally today, another set of institutions has prospered as our politic life has become more volatile and abstract. Each party thrives financially when the other party can be portrayed as extreme, dangerous, even demonic. Wallets don't open when those on the other side are seen as complex, moderate, human, worthy of respect. They open when those on the other side are seen as racists or elitists, abusers or intruders. An enormous infrastructure of political consultants, pollsters, media advisors, direct mail moguls, and academic cheerleaders has grown, while the actual physical infrastructure has declined. The more that politics can be about caricature and imagery and less about engagement and delivery, the better for the ruling class of Americans. Media and publishing empires both feed and profit from this trend, on both ends of the spectrum. The two major parties are as symbiotic as they are polarized.

Modern America no longer works – both literally and figuratively – for the majority of its citizens. But it does work the two polarized parties. It does work for the top 1% of income earners – increasingly in the finance and finance-related professions. It does work for the elite schools at all levels that serve as seminaries for this modern royalty or clerisy. It does work for those who administer redundant government agencies and authorities and institutions. And it has worked and still barely works for those public sector employees who staff society's largest educational, penal, and security systems. Like a chronically failing school system, our current polarized condition works for many of the paid professionals and cost-plus contractors and do-nothing service providers but fails the majority of the recipients of service. It rewards the powerful self-serving parts, while undermining the loosely organized and less powerful whole.

Many people worry that those involved in the Tea Party Movement and other conservative efforts are too aggressive or extreme. I would argue that they have, thus far, been too passive or distracted. The Tea Party defenders of negative liberty (*freedom from*) haven't been too "radical." They haven't been radical enough, or they have aimed their anger at smaller and softer targets. They are like the white homeowners in West Garfield Park in Chicago or the formerly stable neighborhoods of Milwaukee: they are fighting an immediate "enemy" who doesn't look like them, while the mayors and aldermen, real estate agents and mortgage brokers, title companies and hustler lawyers laugh all the way to the bank.

If the Tea Partiers were more radical, they would track the trajectory of the Midwest and see it for what it is: a warning to the nation. Outside of the islands of prosperity along the Chicago lakefront and in places like Columbus, Ohio; Madison, Wisconsin; and Ann Arbor, Michigan; the Midwest has gone from bread basket to basket case. It can be viewed as one vast impoverished Chicago west side – characterized by job loss, population loss, equity loss, institutional decline, extending through five decades, as far as the eye can see. If you can't take your own personal tour, follow the one provided by Richard C. Longworth in his sensitive and sobering account of what happened to an entire region. For every Evanston, there are scores of struggling places like Rockford and Beardstown. For every Columbus, many more Lorains and Daytons. For every Ann Arbor, more Hamtramcks and Flints. His book is titled *Caught In The Middle*, which aptly describes the condition and location of more and more Americans.

Rebuilding a region, or a nation, is beyond the ability of Glenn Beck or Jon Stewart, the polarized Democratic or the polarized Republican parties. The Tea Partiers may feel and appreciate this at a much deeper level than most progressives, who are largely professionals living in the few islands of prosperity that remain.

★★★★

In organizing, we teach that great and thriving institutions do three things: they provide people with opportunities to relate publicly and purposefully; they design ways for people to learn together, satisfying the enormous appetite for knowledge and improvement that seems wired into our DNA; and they engage their members in meaningful public action. Relating, learning, and acting – when a congregation, or association, or party, or community, or country hits on all three of these cylinders, it can really move forward. When it misses on one or more, it either lumbers or stalls or goes into reverse.

The Tea Party crowd deserves credit. In the face of what many pundits predicted was a tidal and long-term leftward shift in American politics in the presidential election of 2008, they didn't sulk. They went to work. They ranged out and related to people who didn't believe that the election represented some second coming. They mobilized citizens with remarkable effectiveness. That means they had to listen to people, meet with them, host house meetings, go door-to-door and development-to-development. As effective as they have been however, they are now in for a tougher challenge. Let's see if they are willing to go the next step and go face to face with those less likely to agree with them on everything. And let's see if those on the left, who often consider themselves smarter and better-informed, are willing to follow the woman in central Illinois into people's dens and basements and hear what they have to say. Old Mayor Daley used to rail, "It's easy to criticize. But where are your programs?" The same is true today. It's easy to criticize. But where are your followers? Where are you building new relationships?

What about learning? One of the great points of tension in the nation is the debate over who we are as a people and how we were formed. Those on the left often assume that those on the right are yahoos, but I would argue that those on the right may be closer to the earliest and deepest rhythms of the nation. Those on the left, in other words, have a lot to learn. And their willingness to stop moralizing long enough to engage those who value *freedom from* more highly, to acknowledge the wisdom of this form of freedom, and to respect those who espouse it, would be a start. Without that, without a basic respect for the political intelligence of ordinary people, there is no possibility of a genuine and reciprocal relationship ever forming. The left would be shocked to learn that most Americans aren't waiting breathlessly to be enlightened by them.

But those on the right have something to learn as well. They have a sophisticated and historically rich *ideological* analysis, but they have a much more limited *power* analysis. The unfettered market that they promote is corroding the freer society they seek to create. The government that they understandably doubt sometimes generates a benefit or support, like Social Security, that helps make that community and society possible. Someone can remain basically conservative and skeptical of bigger government while still acknowledging that reality. One can remain conservative and patriotic, but express profound concern about the unaccountable growth of the nation's homeland security operations and facilities – a vast and expensive expansion of governmental structures and forms of intrusion. This is the greatest threat to those who appreciate the value and wisdom of *freedom from*.

At the same time, someone can remain progressive and devoted to better government while still admitting the failure and limitations of many of its programs – like the Job Training Partnership Act that trained 100,000 cosmetologists one year, about 90,000 more than were needed, or the New York City Board of Education that generated administrative jobs by the thousands in central and "local community" bureaucracies. One can remain progressive and realize that your most prized institutions – elite private and public universities – have sold out to corporate and security industries because that's where the bucks and highest-paying jobs are today.

What can we learn – right, left, and middle – *together*? We can learn how to dis-organize and re-organize our school systems – not to satisfy a simplistic market theory or to protect an inert governmental bureaucracy but to identify and multiply the best practices from all camps in the interests of our students and their futures. We can learn what it takes to recreate productive capacity – *making things* – in our cities and towns and counties. If Andy Grove could figure out how to create Intel and keep (at least for a while) most of the production work in the United States, why can't 50 or 500 or 5,000 Andy Groves do the same? Why isn't government funding focused on this core value?

And what can we do – how can we *act* – together? Even if people are in different camps and believing in very different values, for the growing number of Americans who are increasingly isolated, disconnected, and un-engaged the very act of contending with one another is a kind of common action. The rich and complex fabric of relationships once woven by local religious, political, labor, and business institutions is badly frayed. Reweaving those relationships and reinforcing that fabric, no matter which side of an argument or election campaign someone is on, would be an enormous feat. We are less and less one nation and more a collection of factions, entitlements, regions, and movements with each passing year.

We need to work – and generate work – together. The magic bullet of the right – the market – and the magic bullet of the left – government transfer payments and limited incentives – have both fallen short. In my middle class family, more adults are unemployed than employed – some unemployed for years, a few wondering if they will ever work again. Several who remain employed have already lost one job and found another – with less pay and no benefits. In one case, in Chicago, still considered by some a "union town," payday often comes and goes because the employer doesn't have the funds to cut checks. No worker leaves. No one blows the whistle. No one calls the press. No one strikes. Nearly thirty-five years ago my wife and I were visiting San Francisco. An elderly fellow asked us where we were from, and we said we had come from Chicago. "Chicago," he said, holding out his hands, "a man can always find work in Chicago." No longer. And no longer in America. We don't yet know the cost of this new reality, but it will tend to be unbearably high.

When we think of putting millions of people to work, we don't think of America. We think of China. But that's exactly what we have to do. There is work to be done – retrofitting almost every American building to make them more energy efficient, cleaning and improving the areas around our railroads, upgrading thousands of bridges and tunnels and other forms of infrastructure, improving public transit, recreating the tool-and-dye industry, making high-end medical equipment. And there's the capital to invest in productive uses. A New York City colleague, financial expert John McCarthy, claims in a forthcoming essay that pension and insurance funds alone generate $15 trillion dollars in capital that needs to be invested. The only problem is that those who invest those funds seek returns beyond the capacity of longer-term, lower-yielding enterprises. We are a nation with an excess of workers, an excess of capital, and an enormous amount of work to be done, but with no ability to connect these three fundamental realities.

None of these opportunities is *the* answer. Berlin warned about "the conviction that all positive values in which men have believed must, in the end, be compatible, and perhaps even entail one another." We have taken this conviction one step further in recent times. Some politicians and even some religious leaders promote the notion that all positive values can be embodied

– in one person, in a single human brand – as a package of images and promises and sayings. But they contribute nothing to the need to relate and learn and act more collectively and productively. In fact, they distract from addressing these important challenges and delay the start of the social and political recovery that may need to precede our economic one.

AFTERWORD

★★★★

What in the world would make anyone believe that conservatives and progressives and the majority in the middle can break out of the stalemate we are all in?

I sensed at least the beginning of an answer as my wife and I visited Berlin not long ago. We walked all over the city and saw many signs of the Wall – literally. At one place, near the magnificent Hauptbaunhaoff, the new central train station completed in 2006, we spotted a plaque to the memory of Gunter Litfin.

"A few days after the Wall was built, 24-year-old Gunter Litfin tried to flee from East to West Berlin at Humboldtsrasse…. Startled by shouting guards and warning shots, Gunter Litfin tried to escape by leaping into the water. The water belonged to the East; bank opposite belonged to the western part of Berlin. The guards fired a salvo. Then, one of them took aim and shot Gunter Litfin twice in the back of the neck. Gunter

Litfin disappeared. Three hours later, the East German fire brigade pulled the body out of the water. A crowd had followed events from the opposite bank. Gunter Litfin was the first to be intentionally shot at the inner-Berlin border after 13 August 1961. A memorial stone was unveiled on the first anniversary of his death."

It is a simple and moving memorial, right where the bridge meets the then-western bank that Gunter Litfin could see as he dove into the water and heard the shots ring out, with a portion of the wall preserved in the bridge metal work. This place, like the remains of the wall preserved near a cemetery off Invalidenstrasse, reminded me of Gettysburg in many ways – another hallowed ground. "The brave men," Lincoln said, "living and dead, who struggled here, have consecrated it far above our power to add or detract.... It is for us, the living, rather to be dedicated to the unfinished work that they have thus far so nobly carried on....."

We were in Berlin, with my IAF colleague Arnie Graf and his wife, Lucille, to see how modern Germans were carrying on their own unfinished work. We were privileged to participate in an important assembly of the Deutsches Institut for Community Organizing (DICO). In a packed hall in the Wedding district, a few miles from the center of the city, 235 German leaders from Berlin and Hamburg, Wuppertal and elsewhere, came together and launched a training center for community and civic leaders in that country. The United States Ambassador to Germany, Philip Murphy, spoke warmly about the need for civic participation and more organizing at the community level. He even cited what we in the IAF call the iron rule of effective organizing: "never doing for others what they can do for themselves." Three major European foundations committed funding. But, most importantly, German people of all kinds – native, Turkish, Philipino, Bengali, Palestinian, and others – committed to work together to improve life for all in their increasingly diverse and complex communities. We were standing in a city where gold squares mark the former residences of Jewish tenants dragged from their beds to their deaths in concentration camps, where the sides of some buildings are memorialized with the plaques naming the families killed in the camps who once lived normal lives just beyond the walls, where bullet holes from the final battle for the city still pock some plaster and brick, where the concept of a total and final solution was taken to its greatest and most grotesque extreme.

As we walked around the Reichstag on our last night there, workers were assembling the stage and light stands for the upcoming twenty-year anniversary of the formal reunification of modern Germany. The workers moved efficiently in a gentle mist as a long line of people – German school groups, American and European tourists, runners who had competed in the Berlin marathon the day before, and a few people from farther-off corners of the world – waited to climb the stairs and enter the building. It's the place where 1,500 German soldiers made their last stand against the relentless Russian assault, the shock troops of one final solution slaughtering the shock troops of another. It's now place of tourist interest, pragmatic governance, and national pride.

Who could have predicted this? That we would be standing on those steps, sixty-five years after our fathers fought and won a war against the fathers of the crew assembling the stage? Even thirty years ago, few could have foretold the fall of the Berlin Wall, the dissolution of the Soviet Republic, the reunification of the German people – Dem Deutsche Volke, as it said, chiseled into the stone high above our heads – and the formation of the European Union. Fewer still could have guessed that apartheid would end, that Nelson Mandela would survive Robben Island to lead the new South Africa, that New York City would avert bankruptcy and social collapse and be fully reconstructed and revived, or that a man who could not have entered the University of Georgia in 1960 would be elected President of the United States.

Whatever you may think of one or more of these developments, they defy prediction. They bear witness to the resiliency of the human spirit. And they speak to a greater degree of dynamism and creativity in the political and social arena than in the place more commonly credited with these qualities – the market.

At the same time, it's important to say that they are all incomplete. They lack finality or totality. They are all flawed and expensive. They are – have been from the start – denied by some and resisted by others. They are all in process and in need of ongoing reorganizing. Perhaps that's why, for the most part, they have been remarkably free from the violence and mayhem that darkened three-quarters of the last century.

The German people are proving that they are capable of enthusiastically supporting or grudgingly accepting, often with gritted teeth, these profound shifts in their politics and culture. Although it is not a race, I believe that the American people are as well. We are capable of relating to those we don't yet know and often disagree with. We are capable of learning how to tackle fundamental social and economic challenges in new ways. We are capable of acting and producing together again. We are capable of realigning our economy, reigning in both a crippling and self-serving cowboy market and a suffocating and self-serving government bureaucracy, so that it provides long term employment and sustainable prosperity again.

My wife always says to take the long view. That's what mature people do – looking both forward and back. And that's what mature societies do as well.

OTHER RESOURCES ON ORGANIZING

STOKING THE FIRE OF DEMOCRACY
Our Generation's Introduction to Grassroots Organizing
by Stephen Noble Smith
Stephen Smith is a voice from and for the next generation of fighters for social justice. Here he explains how "could-be radicals" can recruit and support new leaders, turn isolated anger into targeted action, and—more than anything—muster the courage to make mistakes and learn from them.
123-page hardcover, $19.95

AFTER AMERICA'S MIDLIFE CRISIS
by Michael Gecan
Michael Gecan paints a vivid picture of civic, political, and religious institutions in decline, from suburban budget crises to failing public schools, what he describes as "a national midlife crisis." He shows how local organizational efforts can create vibrant institutions that truly serve their constituents and preserve and advance their communities.
128-page hardcover, $14.95

ROOTS FOR RADICALS
Organizing for Power, Action and Justice
by Edward T. Chambers
Ed Chambers' description of the "universals" of organizing. Demonstrates how to make connections across differences of nationality, culture and class. Offers practical ideas and examples for the development of citizen and congregational power.
152-pages hardcover, $12.95

AVAILABLE FROM BOOKSELLERS OR CALL 800-397-2282
WWW.ACTAPUBLICATIONS.COM

OTHER RESOURCES ON ORGANIZING

ACTION CREATES PUBLIC LIFE
by Edward T. Chambers

Ed Chambers, the successor to Saul Alinsky and an organizer for over 55 years, mulls about the need for human beings to develop their "Public life." He argues that it is by taking action that we define who we are as adults and help create the world-as-it-could-be. Written for those who want to participate in shaping society rather than sit around and complain about things. 35 pages, paperback, $5.95

THE POWER OF RELATIONAL ACTION
by Edward T. Chambers

Ed Chambers mulls about the building of relationships in public life that allow us to share our values, passions and interests with one another—what he calls "mixing human spirits." He describes the art of the relational meeting or "one-to-one," which he helped developed and which is now being used by clergy, leaders and organizers around the United States and in several other countries to build their congregations and community institutions and to take joint action for the common good. 33-page paperback, $5.95

THE BODY TRUMPS THE BRAIN
by Edward T. Chambers

The executive director of the Industrial Areas Foundation (IAF) looks at how humans learn with all their senses—including instinct and intuition—and how our educations system tries to downplay what he calls "social knowledge" in favor of academic exercises.
48-page paperback, $5.95

AVAILABLE FROM BOOKSELLERS OR CALL 800-397-2282
WWW.ACTAPUBLICATIONS.COM

OTHER RESOURCES ON ORGANIZING

REFLECTING WITH SCRIPTURE ON COMMUNITY ORGANIZING
by Rev. Jeff Krehbiel

The pastor of the Church of the Pilgrims in Washington, D.C., and co-chair of the Washington Interfaith Network offers reflections on four passages from Scripture and how they relate to the experience of community organizing. He also offers a Group Study Guide for congregational use. 60-page paperback, $5.95

EFFECTIVE ORGANIZING FOR CONGREGATIONAL RENEWAL
by Michael Gecan

The author of *Going Public* and co-executive director of the Industrial Areas Foundation describes how the tools of organizing can and are transforming Protestant, Catholic, Jewish and Muslim congregations. Included are five case studies of congregations that have used this process to grow. 54-page paperback, $5.95

REBUILDING OUR INSTITUTIONS
by Ernesto Cortes, Jr.

Ernie Cortes, the co-executive director of the Industrial Areas Foundation, argues that community organizing cultivates the practices needed for democracy to thrive, including one-on-one relational meetings, house meetings, and systematic reflection on them afterwards. This book contains several examples from organizations in California, Louisiana, and Texas that helped local congregations and other mediating institutions identify, confront, and change things that were destroying their families and communities. 30-page paperback, $5.95

AVAILABLE FROM BOOKSELLERS OR CALL 800-397-2282
WWW.ACTAPUBLICATIONS.COM

OTHER RESOURCES ON ORGANIZING

GOING PUBLIC
An Organizer's Guide to Citizen Action
by Michael Gecan

Mike Gecan, the co-executive director of the Industrial Areas Foundation and Metro IAF, tells stories and teaches lessons from his lifetime in community organizing. He explores the difference between "public" and "private," and the critical importance of building relationships as the basis for all successful, long-term organizing. Studs Terkel said, "*Going Public* is one of the most hopeful books I've read in years." 192-page paperback, $12.95

WHAT IS SOCIAL JUSTICE?
by William L. Droel

A primer by Bill Droel of the National Center for the Laity on the difference between social justice and charity, commutative justice, and distributive justice. Explains that social justice is a virtue that is practiced mostly by "insiders" of institutions, sometimes with a little help from "outsiders," and must result in the act of organizing if it is to come to fruition. 42-page paperback, $5.95

ACTIVISM THAT MAKES SENSE
Congregations and Community Organization
by Gregory F. Augustine Pierce

The classic book by Greg Pierce on why community organizing "makes sense" for parishes and congregations. Covers key issues such as self-interest, power, controversy, organization, and leadership development. 148-page paperback, $9.95

AVAILABLE FROM BOOKSELLERS OR CALL 800-397-2282
WWW.ACTAPUBLICATIONS.COM